José Ramón Sánchez Leyva

The Black Arrow

Translated by Esther Whitfield

and Katerina González Seligmann

Barcelona 2024
Linkgua-ediciones.com

Credits

Table of Contents

The author of *The Black Arrow* has lived most of his life in Guantánamo—the city and provincial capital in Eastern Cuba, nine hundred miles from Havana and twenty from the infamous Naval Station at Guantánamo Bay. It is a place separated from much of Cuba by distance, difficult transport, and the political and cultural dominance of the faraway capital city. The city of Guantánamo is also separated from the Naval Station by a land-mined no man's land, a barbed wire fence, and over sixty years of hostile U.S.-Cuba relations. In this collection of poetry, José Ramón Sánchez imaginatively occupies the forbidden space of the Naval Station, along with its history, its borderlands, its prisoners, and its ominous geopolitical significance.

Isolated though it may be, the Guantánamo that the author inhabits in these poems is expansive in its history, geography, and imaginative connections. It is the Guantánamo of long-standing imperialist designs and resistance: of the Spanish-Cuban-American War that ended colonial rule in Cuba and established the continuing American presence at Guantánamo, through the lease in perpetuity that has been a vehement theme in the anti-imperialist rhetoric of the Cuban Revolution since Fidel Castro first seized power. It is the hostile space of the post-1959 years during which the base has been framed as a threat to Cuba, whose military forces surveil a borderland impassable to Cuban citizens other than the few elderly base workers permitted to continue crossing back and forth until the last of them retired in 2012 — and the wild animals who, in several of the author's poems, graze there freely. Also unhindered by the border, until systems were upgraded on the base, were radio and television channels that allowed residents of Cuban Guantánamo to listen into English-language broadcasts unavailable elsewhere in the country, allowing them what the author calls, in "The Channel from the Base," "the exclusive luxury" of "an outside world/ beyond our socialist republic."

Post 9/ 11 Guantánamo, that has held over seven hundred detainees as "enemy combatants", is well-known worldwide but has had a scant presence in the Cuban press. The experience of the detainees — as Muslims, as prisoners, and in many cases as poets—is, however, deeply compelling to the author. He pieces together what he can about this experience from a haphazard and multivocal archive: memories of a childhood in which light, sound, and broadcast signals from the base reached into the surrounding areas; printed histories and maps; official records pertaining to the base's creation and development; oral reports from residents of Guantánamo province; leaked documents pertaining to detention operations; and detainees' poetry.

The poems are written in a documentary style distilled of ornamentation that approximates the sparse style of the Naval Base itself. They are tied up in the combat histories and present of the base, confronting head-on the racial and gendered violence of imperial warfare and torture. Without the adornment of the captivating imagery associated with surrealism, they follow the surrealist principle of creating meaning through the linking of opposites, as the poet suggests with his voicing of Cuban lyric poet Regino Eladio Boti in "Secret// Noforn// 20330602." This principle is again at work in "The Hooked Nose of the Semite," where the author's use of the word "Semite" draws attention to the shared "Semitic" origins of many Jewish and Muslim peoples and the absurdity of the profiling tactics used to capture alleged "enemy combatants." The nose in question is the poet's own, and it highlights both the contradictions of racial profiling and the poet's identification with the prisoners at the base.

Nevertheless, as the author acknowledges in the poem "Impossible," much of what he knows must necessarily come from his own imagination, just as his writing comes from a drive to translate others' experience in terms of his own. Some of the very areas that made the author's poems difficult for his English translators — the word "Semite," for example, and the more general insistence on inhabiting experiences that, on the face of it, are significantly harsher than those of a Cuban poet — give rise to ethical questions about the limits of translation as a practice. And yet the will to think of another's experience in terms of one's own, like the will to usher words from one language into another, is largely empathic: it depends on finding, and feeling, something in common. It is in this spirt that we have read, and translated, *The Black Arrow*.

Katerina González Seligmann
and Esther Whitfield, November 2024

WELCOME TO
U. S. NAVAL STATION
GUANTANAMO BAY, CUBA

WELCOME ABOARD
78°F

The Black Arrow

In the cells of the Muslim prisoners
at the Naval Base there is an arrow
pointing toward Mecca.

The Base is at 19', 54', 42. 95" North
        and 75°, 09', 11. 75" West.
Mecca is at 21°, 25', 01" North
        and 39°, 49', 00" East.

12793 kilometers over the Atlantic
the Sahara and the Red Sea
their prayers must travel:
a minimal geographic impertinence
that will not keep them from Paradise.

And if the Americans
had not provided the arrows
• • • • then
        what?

Castles of Misery

Long distance combat,
portable tourism on a weak internet connection,
photos that pixelate when you enlarge them,
conversations snatched randomly from
Old TV reruns,
documents anyone can read,
childhood memories. Old maps,
a trip to the Malones lookout, almost aborted
and a little imagination, of no consequence.
      (in the "terror mode" activated by extreme situations
          I evacuated from Kittery Beach
without understanding what the sign said) ./ You have this
  much:
          you are worth this much in the prison of poetry.
         Scarcity that doesn't kill you nourishes you.
Too well-nourished, you lose the urge to invent what you
  need.
             Scarcity justifies poetry.
        Misery's frail castles stand justified.

The Channel from the Base

The channel from the Base was one of Cumberland's luxuries
until the late 1990s.
An exclusive luxury in this country:
we could watch the Major Leagues live
and know that there was an outside world
beyond our socialist republic.

Most of all I remember "El Duque" Hernández
pitching for the New York Yankees:
slider after slider, a guaranteed win.
He was our man in New York.

Guantánamo Bay Cuba was its tag line.
Another way to break the embargo.
A small-scale myth. An endangered legend.

Impossible

It's impossible to write about the base with no direct
  experience.
I never wanted to leave on a raft, and some time ago I
  exhausted
what little news I had.
As I have no direct experience
I write second-hand poetry.
I take the words of others, images others saw for me
and enclose them in a verbal formula with a simple rhythm,
in a simple and schematic square of prose.
I will never enter the base. Writing poetry based on
  documents
is like basing your sex life on masturbation.
The barbed wire cuts inside and out.

Spotlight

Sometimes at night news   would
reach us from the   Base:
a stream of white   light
through the flame tree   blossoms
a small-scale spectacle
in the line at the   dining   hall
a distraction amid our   misfortune.

Perhaps the light was   ours
but malcontents take pleasure
in the danger of   foreign   lights.

Foreign lights mixed up   with   ours
and scrutinized us without   compassion.

In between the streams   of white   light
we survived as a   distraction.

GOOD LUCK SAILORS & MARINES
DON'T LEAVE CUBA BEFORE HAVING A CRISTAL
BEER
TO REMIND YOU OF GUANTANAMO HAVE A GOOD
TIME DRINKING TROPICAL BEER

A Trojan Horse in the Caribbean

Fight your own war:
    today's ally
    will soon become
    your worst enemy.
(Stephen Crane says
    that the Mambises[1]
    were grateful to the gringos:
    people with good horses
    who despised black people.)
The naïve Mambises were unable to control
    the help they received,
    and the helpers took over
    the leading role themselves.
Guantánamo was special due to its conditions,
    but if it had not been Guantánamo
    they would have taken anything else.
Guantánamo is the jewel of our compromise,
    The price for keeping the Spanish
    away forever.
The end of sugar tourism in the Caribbean.
Go find brown women in Morocco.
Come back later,
    when the Euro has lengthened your whip
    and makes us happy.
Surprised once, surprised twice.
The heroic Mambises could only fight

---

1   The pro-independence milita, the majority of which was made up of
formerly enslaved Black soldiers, has been colloquially referred to
collectively as los mambíses.

against an obvious enemy:
after all
it is not easy to resist such a beautiful horse.

The Hooked Nose of the Semite

The Semite's hooked nose
is the hooked nose of the poet
who with the money (scarce)
from the (indecent) poems
bought himself a Casio F-91W watch
and a black unbranded knife
in the shops of Caracas.

Enough to be returned to Gitmo
with enemy combatant status
on either side of the fence.

He knew he was guilty of the knife and the poems.
    He did not know that Casios
    identified members of Al-Qaeda.

Any distortion of obedience
(a knife, a watch, a packet of indecent poems)
can prompt your death sentence.
    The knife in its sheath,
    the Casio out of batteries,
    the hooked nose
looking for trouble.

Small Change

Oscar Cruz compares me to the prisoners at Guantánamo
  Bay:
isolation, mistreatment, scarcity and other endearments.

It's impossible to write "from above."
You can only express that you're screwed.

Even as you triumph
your words won't be worth a cent.

(They say that marines on leave
would fill their pockets with small change

to throw to the children).
Until I have enough small change

I will be a Taliban in writing:
Isolation, mistreatment, scarcity and other beatings.

DANGER
THIS AREA PATROLLED
BY VICIOUS DOGS

PELIGRO
ESTA AREA PATRULLADA
POR PERROS BRAVOS

Malones

Sometimes I'm asked for news about the base.
There is no news (I answer).

We know what the papers tell us
and what we hear through the grapevine, our local network

Anyone who wants more will have to cross the fence line.
The wall I scaled was insignificant:

I only saw the car headlights
and the wake a ferry left in the sea.

Camp Death stood out for its absence.

They called the sunset "beautiful,"
but I can't paint the ecosystem.

BEWARE
JET INTAKE
JET BLAST
PROPELLERS

KILLERS
LEEWARD POINT

Bird of Passage

Stephen Crane was at Cumberland
at the end of the nineteenth century. A correspondent

for the Spanish-Cuban-American War.
(Look up what he wrote about this).

An elevation named after him in the southern
part of the bay is the only toponym

on the archipelago named for a poet.
Other than José Martí. Who is also the only poet found on
  currency.

The Chant

Hey hey, ho ho:
Caimanera's got to go!

Hey hey, ho ho:
the Naval Base has got to go!

(Until we learned
that Caimanera

was also ours).

"Hey hey, ho ho:
exile scum have got to go!

Hey hey, ho ho:
the Naval Base has got to go!"

(Until we learned that
the exile scum

were also ours).

"The Naval Base has got to go!"
(Until it becomes ours).

Donkey Meat

After completing a day's work
they gave us donkey meat to eat:

it was juicy and had that special taste
of meat raised in the wilderness.

And even though the soldiers are not vegetarians
the local fauna is reserved for wartime.

The local fauna does not mind the hypocrisy
of prospering among people who love to eat steak.

Whoever wants donkey meat knows
where to go when the war begins.

Whoever wants a war can go find
donkey meat at the border.

CAMP JUSTICE
474th Expeditionary Civil Engineer Squadron
Guantánamo Bay, Cuba
"Engineers Lead the Way"

Green Area: A Tour

"The mule's step is a step," Frog's Mouth quoted
nasally, as he rode a Yutong bus.

The border donkeys watched us
knowing what we were: bookish tourists.

With what donkey-like zeal they would kick us
until the poems spilled out.

The best-kept animals
of the country live here.

Lodgers of the differential
Imperialism/ Revolution.

Nothing more freeloading than life in the wild.
Mules live in the poem.

Enmity can be ecological.
Donkeys reproduce their freedom.

Virgin Lands

We always heard that the country's
virgin lands were in Baracoa.

Not planted by anyone, this wilderness,
owed its continuity only to itself.

And dreaming about these lands purified those of us
the impoverished city engendered.

Over on the base there is land
that has remained virginal for a very long time:

the day they take down the fence, we will know.
Any unreachable site is a virgin

if you cannot possess it. For the wilderness to grow
it must remain untouched.

Animal Planet

Velásquez set pigs free in the wilderness
and the pigs fattened to their hearts' content.

They did the same, later, with
deer and other game.

The goat heads for the mountain and we
make the wilderness our pantry.

Four centuries later came the Treaty:
"The areas of land occupied by the Naval Station

shall be perfectly delimited
and their limits marked by barbed wire fences;

and all traffic between Cuban territory and the Base
shall be absolutely prohibited from dusk until dawn."

Animals, by night and by day,
were oblivious to the President's orders.

Nor do banana rats and iguanas need
A zoo smaller than the whole archipelago.

It's better to be hunted freely
than protected in cages of obedience.

Guamá[2]

They found me and I knew immediately
they would name me Guamá, the orphaned manatee,

son of the defeated heroes of all wars ever fought
I didn't put up a fight: good behavior gets you

strokes on the belly and nonsense in a funny voice
that speaks in orders, playing nice

because it costs nothing. An endangered species,
they'll send me back to Gitmo if I adapt to life in the wild

and they don't have to force-feed me.
I, who had adapted to living in the wild with no borders.

2   Guamá is the name of one of Eastern Cuba's Taíno leaders and the
     name given to an orphaned manatee rehabilitated in Puerto Rico af-
     ter being found at the Guantánamo Naval Base in 2012.

ALL VISITORS
CHECK IN TO
WORK CONTROL TENT

**DEPARTMENT OF DEFENSE
HEADQUARTERS, JOINT TASK FORCE
GUANTANAMO U. S. NAVAL STATION,
GUANTANAMO BAY, CUBA APO AE 09360[3]**

JTF-GTMO-CDR   2 June 2008

MEMORANDUM FOR Commander, United States Southern Command, 3511 NW 91st Avenue, Miami, FL 33172

SUBJECT: Recommendation for Continued Detention Under DoD Control (CD) for Guantanamo Detainee, ISN US9YM-000030DP (S)

JTF-GTMO Detainee Assessment

1. (S) Personal Information:

- JDIMS/ NDRC Reference Name: <u>Regino Eladio Boti Barreiro</u>
- Current/ True Name and Aliases: <u>I too, like the soldier-poet from Fiume</u>
- Place of Birth: <u>to the land of Guayo the cacique</u>
- Date of Birth: <u>to my mother, to my sisters, to my nephews</u>

---

3   This poem draws on the rubric of the U.S. Department of Defense's "Detainee Assessment Briefs," classified documents purporting to contain intelligence on detainees held at the Guantánamo detention centers. Sánchez has filled the DAB's information fields with lines from the poetry collection El Mar y la Montaña (1921), by the Cuban poet Regino Eladio Boti y Barreiro.

and nieces

- Citizenship: <u>to my deceased sister/ to my buried father/ to all my dead</u>
- Internment Serial Number (ISN): <u>to all my people between/ the sea and the mountain/ this song from my native farmland/ I do consecrate</u>

2. (U// FOUO) Health: No one should nor could read this book ▆▆▆▆▆▆▆▆ without the gift of becoming more beautiful through the attachment to beings, things and souls.

3. (U) JTF-GTMO Assessment:

a. (S) Recommendation: No one should nor could read this book, ▆▆▆▆▆▆▆▆ without the virtue of associating ideas by linking apparently opposed meanings to uncover unforeseen quarries of light in the subsoil of writing.

b. (S// NF) Executive Summary: Those who can and should read this book will do so ▆▆▆▆▆▆▆▆, many times over.

- until by involuntary amplifications they fill with Amazons and Saharas,
- with Pacifics and Andes, the tortured syntheses that are its pages.
- Those who can and should read this book know that it is an anonymous work: ▆▆▆▆▆▆▆▆

c. (S// NF) Summary of Changes: And that in matters of aesthetics and rhythm it is better to say and do nothing, because everything is already said and done.

- Those who can and should read this book,

- after tasting it, should throw it into the fire;
- — " ███ " —
- because in their spirit there will remain, wandering, the intimate conviction that our language
- as a transmitter of ideas and feelings,
- and as an artistic expression, is a coarse and miserable vessel,
- unable, in its narrowness and crudeness, to contain nuance and emotion.
- Amen.

4. (U) Detainee's Account of Events:

Ancestor of the mountain,/ nurse of the ancient forest/ your core is still/ marvelous

a. (S// FN) Prior History: In the agatine afternoon—/███—/ you hear your mermaids sing/ behind the lateen sail.

b. (S// NF) Recruitment and Travel: Eternal rhythm ███/ you who symphonize lamentations and barcaroles/ your secret saltwater word/ amid the panicked noise of the seashells.

c. (S// NF) Training and Activities: Like a dark-winged, rough-hewn stone/ the kingfisher drops to the sea;/ out of the clear crystal of the waters/ arise two wings ███/ of ephemeral white.

5. (U) Capture Information:

a. (S// NF) The wind threshes its necklace of sounds;/ the sea symphonizes its convulsions/ beneath the baton of the tide

b. (S) Property Held:

- fog layers the bay
    - with green and slate; the rain shower
    - tints the horizon with blue and steel.
  - A sailboat thrusts its prow through a channel
    - Its triangular sail, its light flashing in vain,
    - they awaken the route of the Roman triumvirate;
    - and a vision of love and orgies

c. (S) Transferred to JTF-GTMO: bewitched this summer morning: ▓▓▓ naked below the jewels,/ the triclinium, the spasm, the falsehood/ of the kiss.../ And the kiss of the asp/ The agony.

d. (S// NF) Reasons for Transfer to JTF-GTMO: Somber and luminous rays./▓▓▓: the posts. ▓▓▓: the beach,/ the rails and the rockpools. The day/ pre-agonizes. Sunset softens/ the greys with its roses. In the saltmarsh/ the windmill ▓▓▓, is a dahlia/ gigantic and gyrating. And in the Angelus prayer is a noise/ like the sound made by the wings of Victory.

6. (S// NF) Evaluation of detainee's Account: ▓▓▓; your misanthropic/ tomb is on the leeward cliff./ A broad, black granite cross/ commemorates you. Beneath your tomb rumbles/ the orchestra of the sea, a seashell in the wind;/ but you are not of the infinite./ The sea cliff will turn/ your broad, black, granite cross to dust/ and take you to Scotland, being a wave of the sea./▓▓▓: then you will once again/ enter the heart of the infinite...

7. (U) Detainee Threat:

a. (S) Assessment: In the coffee table marble/ that the sea forms, the red lantern of the twisting boat, is the eye/ ███ that,/ drunk, at the bottom of its cup/ sees its conflagration flicker.

b. (S// NF) Reasons for Continued Detention: From the South comes the rainshower,/ ████;/ it comes erasing mountains,/ it comes swallowing the sea./ From the South comes the rainshower,/ ████;/ the bay is a grey tarp on which everything has faded./ From the South comes the rain shower,/ ☐☐☐☐☐/ falling in somber cloaks/ among which all that can be seen/ is the mass of a schooner/ white like a Spitzberg

- ████/ The voices of silence on the mountain;/ the rhapsodies of the sea; the rattling/ of the wind on the beaches and crags;/ the monastic rhythm of the dead of night;/ the lamentation of the valleys and ravines;/ the aqueous boiling of the seashell/
  - (S// NF) and the symphonizings of the pine trees/ are the groans, cries, ayes and clamors/ of simple and perennial things.
  - (S// NF) They are the chords of the world's pain,/ that the world has a soul
  - (S// NF) ████ a sister/ to our poor human soul
  - (S// NF) A crest of madness,/ remnants of another sad soul/ that lived for dead ages/ a literary cult,/ piety for what exists,/ (████)/ pride and illusion: I.
- (S// NF) ██ chisel my diamond,/ I am my diamond.
  - (S// NF) While others cry/ ██ I stay mute I cut, I chisel;
  - (S// NF) I make *art in silence.*/ And while others are unsettled

- (S// NF) by the rhythms I battle/ and I do not negotiate my name.
- (S// NF) I am my diamond,/■ I chisel my diamond,
- (S// NF) ■■■ I make *art in silence.*
- (S// NF) The entire cosmos is within me./ At dawn, ■■■■,/ the moon and garden keep me company./ A distant noise that I recall, a noise/ audacious and propelling.
- (S// NF) I inquire/ also with my gaze. In the browning/ handful of papers a butterfly/■■■■, with the same noise/ distant, very distant, as an airplane/ on its cautious march.

(S// NF) There is in the nickeling/ at the base of the armchair—/■■■—/ two eyes where a white light—/■■■—has come to rest;/ and on its somber brow/ the exploding bloom/ of an oblong pupil/ where blocks of emerald/ alternate with weed-yellow/ and it is like the conscience of the room

- (S// NF) Created by blows of the chisel/ in proper eminence and under the sun,/ you fly without wings, because/—■■■— you are ideal.
- (S// NF) Graceful, weightless, serene,/ your Hellenic regularity redeems/ from venal mercantilism—■■■—/ the village of my birth.
  - (S// NF) ■■■ How is the mountain/ beautiful? When it is blue distance/ when — setting its core on fire—/ the night is alight/ and the day vibrates in greens?/■■■ How is the mountain/ beautiful?/ It is beautiful from its core/ and rendered blue distance,/ when the night is stars/ and the green spectrum of

the day/ disembowels in flowers/ the green
scale of day.

- (S// NF) In the ruins of the wall and the dam/
stone and water grow old/██████/ their grey
hair green.

- (S// NF) An unexpected gurgling rises up/███
██,/ and, rousing freshness/██,/ it laughs,
sings, moves away, slumbers:/ pain of the
forest, long for it,/ soul of the countryside,
dream.

- (S// NF) The horizon closes—████./ The
glowing clods of earth begin to open up/ The
leaves sparkle. The dewdrops dance/ and the
earth rises ████;/ scent of woman, of tomb
and of bed,/ of kisses and branches, of life,/
of everything, of nothing...

- (S// NF) I am consumed by fever. In the hut/ chat-
ter jumps around.

- (S// NF) But a waft/ of water makes me shiv-
er, and at this carelessess/

- (S// NF) I bundle into my cape./ I drink down
the cup of coffee.

- (S// NF) And the dalliance of my flesh razes/
the carnal scum.

- (S// NF) ████████, I dream/ with my eyes open
and without faith.

- (S// NF) ██████—/ *the burst of dead stone—*

- (S// NF) is ovary and papyrus in its bareness.

- (S// NF) Plant, man, and demos

- (S// NF) Cryptograms show us

- (S// NF) that beings from other stars came to
engrave.

c. (S// NF) **Detainee's Conduct:** A giant ████████/ unites heaven and earth./ A chrysanthemum-yellow strip/ adorns the horizon. In the distance/ the oil lamp of a hut. And then/ lowlands and highlands ████/ black as jet/ like the eternal.

8. (U) Detainee Intelligence Value Assessment:

a. (S) **Assessment:** The udder has four teats/ and the human hand has five fingers./ The stream of milk—████—/ full of white ████ the morning./ And all the men drink from the milk./ How gentle the cow's eyes are!

b. (S// NF) **Placement and Access:** Amid the siena color ████████/ smelling of ████ dung/ the chicken's crests ████/ are poppies,/ the flies ████ are sparks/ the ants are coal.

c. (S// NF) **Intelligence Assessment:** Perhaps the same one ████/ with creation in the pupils;/ but it copies with a melancholy so deep/ so wise and so subtle/ that—████—/ while it ruminates on the Sorites paradox/ it makes poetry with roses and lemon blossom.

d. (S// NF) **Areas of Potential Exploitation:**

- The painful sorrows of the night
- have fallen. The moon barely shines.
- Beneath its luckless mother of pearl
- are outlined the baleful overhangs
- of the rural church. A tower
- crowns the zigzag of its outline
- as a ruined castle. It looks like a slow wagon

- clambering to a senile height.

9. (S) EC Status: And tomorrow, like the ass pulling a waterwheel,/ the mean and somber return/ put down my head and write:/███████,/ with my eyes still ablaze,/ enchanted on an amethyst sea.

J. R. Sánchez
Unreal Poet, Joturia
Donnadie

CLASSIFIED BY: EL MAR Y LA MONTAÑA (VERSÍCULOS INDEMNES)
REASON: *C'est vers la sérénité/ que nous devons tendre.* (RODIN)
DECLASSIFY ON: 11 de julio de 1919-19 de agosto de 1920

CAMP DELTA - 1

MAXIMUM SECURITY
"HONOR BOUND TO DEFEND FREEDOM"

Cell

Table, chair, bed,
Qu'ran, an arrow

pointing to Mecca.
It moves so quickly

that it seems still:
the Americans

can't stand it.

Next Station

And on the recreation yard
there is also an arrow,

showing the prisoners
the great goodwill of their captors:
more active in their faith than the *ulamas*.
And beneath the arrow One Word:

Mecca.

And once again the exact figure-
of pedantic impertinence.

All Rights Reserved

It is also the painstaking realization of the bureaucrat
with a job guaranteed for life and a clear conscience
for having earned it.

If we have to paint arrows we'll paint them,
and signs that say:

SILENCE.

IT IS TIME
FOR PRAYER.

And we'll add this to the payroll:
who knows which perpetual enemy will make us retire?

DETAINEES
IN VICINITY

MAINTAIN SILENCE

The Cow

Faith is instant or it's nothing. Faith or nothing.
What does a distance of 13000 kilometers (or almost)
   matter to faith?

It makes no difference whether you are next to the Cube or
   on the other side of the world.
A little faith is worth more than all the geographic details
   in the world.

From the bottom of a hole prayer will find its way.
Faith is a Mecca whose center is anywhere:

"To Allah belong the East and the West
so withersoever you turn, there will be the face of Allah

Surely, Allah is Bountiful, All-Knowing."[4]
But thirty ayahs later it's contradicted:

 "Verily, we see thee turning thy face often to heaven;
surely, then, will We make thee turn to the Qiblah

which thou likest.
So, turn thy face towards the Sacred Mosque;

And wherever you be, turn your faces towards it."
Faith is a dog nourished by whatever they throw at it.

4   *The Holy Qur'an*, translated by Maulawi Sher'Ali. Islam Interna-
    tional Publications Limited. 2015. Chapter 2, "Al-Baqarah," verses
    116 and 145.

High Infidelity

I don't need your diabolical internet:
your underwater cable, or whatever,

you can stick them up your ass.
I only want my faith and the sharp

tip of an narrow.
Their ridiculous, shark-proof cable

is the ultimate avatar of their misery.
My faith is in Paradise and it is so strong

that I don't need their help.
Mecca is where faith sustains itself.

Alquibla

Although ritual is useful to faith,
too much ritual produces situations

that break what's absolute in belief.
Oh, the whole Earth is sacred

Oh, faith gets caught up in details
that affirm and disorient.

Ritual will fill up with exceptions
every time faith is put to the test.

Faith will empty itself of ritual
When we feel the true orientation.

Circulation

Although Mecca is the target of all the arrows
every prayer returns the plea to its origin.

The boomerang prayer:
it comes from behind and turns, those who plead,

into their own opposites.
Even when the planet has been scorched,

beyond the capacity for life,
these prayers will keep circulating

like a sanctity belt
to be released when the earth explodes.

If the planet were other than it is (flat)
prayers would never return to their origin:

they would stay, archived, in the Kaaba,
or on the loose, drifting. So that they may return,

Prayers must circulate.

If it were flat, we would call it round
And worry about something else.

North-South+East-West

And at the center of the cross, an evasion,
ellipses, free territory, belonging to no-one,

a world without laws, invented by crooked lawyers,
zero-degree coordinates

that determine the
statutes of men without rights,

faithful to the scales where the world is weighed,
a step that crosses the abyss:

you neither live nor die,
you live discreetly in captivity,

you die when it suits them.

360 degrees of ignominy
wherever you are.

Joint Detention Group
Value of the Week

LOYALTY

Joint Detention Group
Value of the Week

RESPECT

Admiral in Chief, Commit Our Suicide

On 9 June 2006, three prisoners killed themselves at Gitmo.
Our acts of war are pure asymmetry.

So asymmetrical that they can barely be identified.
If we all killed ourselves, we would leave power without
  arguments.

The crime is also called "suicide."
Living is pretending you can do it, but without knowing it.

The Narrow Gate

The best paid workers in the country
passed through the gate meekly.

Thousands of times they crossed over and now
they wait to be paid what they are owed.

They lived in a bubble and only abandoned it
to go and sleep with their little ones.

There they were called "communists," and here they get
  called "nasty old men."
The nasty communists survive the friction of the tides.

The Form of the Bay

Wide and deep, like a body trespassed thousands of times.
In the upper part, small-scale fishermen, infected fish.

In the lower part, warships, high quality tuna.
An unstoppable flow, oblivious to treaties.

Indiscreetly swaying waters that seek permanent orgasm.
Until the tide rises and covers the valley, it will be a
  disputed body.

What the sea permitted, the sea will make impossible again.
The border is the sea, not the fence land-mined by a lease.

OFF LIMITS
TRESPASSERS
WILL BE
PROSECUTED
By Order of Commander. JTF

Short Message

Novice poets like all of us,
the Muslim prisoners can barely see their surroundings.

Writing is less a sign of self-liberation
than of good prison conditions.

Build yourself a prison of words
and you will more easily forget the prison around you.

If it convinces you
others' condemnation won't matter.

And what poems do the Marines
who guard them write?

A poem called "Waterboarding"
and one called "Force-feeding."

[I'm good honey: I beat the truth
out of 1 Saracen today].

Although power prefers prose,
if he gets randy he sends verses.

It's not the same to come into a Nokia
as into little polystyrene cups.

They Are Very Close

You either become more forward or lose all shame.
A visit every two minutes won't allow for more.

An interrupted jerk-off is as unpleasant
as a mirage in the middle of the desert.

Any day, every two minutes,
my wrist can create a mirage.

I am going to bestow on the snitch of mirages
the hottest part of the desert.

The gaze that cuts me off deserves
the unstoppable flow of satisfaction.

Mental masturbation is not impossible
for someone who lives in the desert.

Even a well-delivered dry boarding
can seem attractive:

sex life is a power
nourished by straying.

Infinite days in Camp Delta
or

¿How can you be a complete man,
on the basis of jerk-offs, waterboarding, and prayers?

NO HAT
NO SALUTE
AREA

Dry Boarding

If you can manage maximum concentration
(your mind blank lest thinking rob you of your oxygen)

you may last two minutes underwater.
And although a constant stream is worse

than a stable mass of liquid
the training will be good for something.

If you can manage to avoid the context
you will not suffer the anguish of asphyxiation:

you will navigate the submarine you have become.
Apnea, liberating us from ballast,

approximates contemplation and dry boarding
(if you don't yield to the struggle that will rob you of
  oxygen)

approximates a convulsive spiritual exercise.
The believer who dies in the submarine is a martyr to the
  divine.

Hunger Strike

According to their enemies, the Muslim prisoners
go on hunger strike
to get attention from the media.

Going hungry is a condition of poetry.
The prisoner is an artist of freedom.
Going hungry to achieve freedom

is a condition of poetry.
The prisoner who endures hunger to achieve
the condition of poetry is an artist of freedom.

To go hungry to achieve poetry
is a condition of freedom.
It is a condition of freedom to go hungry

for poetry. Poetry and freedom
do not cure hunger, but they do use it.
The prisoner is an artist of hunger

who achieves the (conditional) freedom of poetry.
The (conditional) freedom of poetry
is also a method of asymmetrical warfare.

"I am dying alive."
"They are tying me down by force."
"It seems that Guantanamo

is going backwards."

"I will not eat again
until they return my dignity."

If your poems keep failing
you can take your strike to the next level.
Living is pretending you can do it, but without knowing it.

NO PHOTOGRAPHY

Opening the Screen

Opening the screen that removes me from the world
of captivity in which I live, the first thing I see,
after entering my password,

is an enclosed metallic room
a prisoner's comfortable cage.
From one captivity to another nothing changes

and every day I connect two captivities.
The screen brings me back in the afternoon
tired and less free than the last time.

The screen reflects my face watching another prison.
Watching the screen that reflects my face
I see two prisons at once. In the top left

corner of the cage
a convex triangular mirror shows
the blind spot behind us.

DO NOT FEED
WILDLIFE / IGUANAS.

The Desert Man

The desert man is not humanized.
He is shut up with all his rights removed,
except his right to be an "enemy combatant."
The care provided for the desert man
is the care given to raving madmen
and serial killers: hands and feet
in chains, surveillance every three minutes,
solitary confinement, and death-row uniforms.
Such a protocol is the apex
of Western Christian humanism:
the freedom to fight convenient wars
by any means necessary.
The desert man, vanquished,
survives in his enemy's comfort.
Guantánamo is the maximum hospitality
they can offer him: one million
dollars a year, and the sum is on the rise,
for an incalculable number of years.
When we all become "enemy combatants"
there will be no such extravagance.

Collateral Damage

We are and we are not here.
We are and are not from this place.
We know this is an enemy military base
in the free territory of a republic that once produced sugar.

We come to work, spend time
with our relatives and learn to be
that impossible thing, that illegal trauma that judges
cannot resolve without causing more conflict:
                                        a gitmo
                        (half Cuba, half United States).
A species as rare as a fairy-tale troll.

Migrant birds in a sterile land
we mimic civil life among the weapons.
Women and children of nomadic desert
tribes must have felt the same way.

The desert, like always, has grown.
The world is an enemy military base.
Any territory is free to be conquered.
Collateral damage is happening constantly.

The Infinite Fence

What is a base if not one island inside another?
What is an island if not a country with no need for borders
because it has the perfect boundary,
that opens out in all directions and in its movement
smooths out an endless finish to the land?
And what is the planet if not a base
leased to us with no guarantees?
What the sea chipped away at, we keep chipping away.
What space delivers to us, we will enjoy.
We will relinquish the base, we will relinquish the island,
we will relinquish the Earth. We will jump to another
  planet,
another island fenced in by weightlessness.
The universe is an expanding base
and its fence is an uncreated space,
where suns will explode like mines
and a black hole at the center of the galaxies
will define the status of our enemies.

LEAVING
U. S. NAVAL
BASE